DESERT STORM

The Gulf War 1990-1991

JOHN PERRITANO

Editor Phyllis Baecker
Publishing Director Chester Fisher
Client Service Manager Ravneet Kaur
Art Director Sumit Charles
Senior Designer Joita Das
Project Manager Shekhar Kapur
Art Editor Amit Prashant Tigga
Picture Researcher Kamal Kumar

10 9 8 7 6 5 4 3 2 1

ISBN: 81-905723-1-8

Printed in China

Picture Credits

Cover Images : Front (All): DoDmedia
Back : DoDmedia

Half title: Gunnery Sgt. Mark Oliva : U.S. Marines

Content Images :

Patrick de Noirmont : Reuters. DoDmedia

4-5 DoDmedia. 6-7 DoDmedia. 8-9 Michael Zysman : Shutterstock. 9 Peter Jordan : Alamy. 11 Associated Press. 13 Visions of America, LLC : Alamy. 14-15 DoDmedia. 16 Associated Press. 17t TebNad : Shutterstock.17b Tal Delbari : Shutterstock.18 DoDmedia. 19 DoDmedia. 20-21 DoDmedia. 21t Associated Press.

22 DoDmedia. 23t Patrick de Noirmont : Reuters. 24-25 U.S. Air Force photo : Master Sgt. Lance Cheung. 25t DoDmedia. 25b DoDmedia. 27 Rex Features. 27 (inset) Associated Press. 28 DoDmedia. 29t Associated Press. 30 Associated Press. 31 Associated Press. 32-33 DoDmedia. 34 DoDmedia. 37 Associated Press.

CONTENTS

"LIVE FROM BAGHDAD"

On January 17, 1991, the early morning sky was clear and dark. The crescent of a new moon hung over the Persian Gulf in the Middle East. At about 2:35 a.m., explosion after explosion rocked the ancient city of Baghdad, the capital of Iraq.

"The skies over Baghdad have been illuminated," reported CNN news correspondent Bernard Shaw. Millions had tuned in to watch the beginning of the Persian Gulf War unfold live on TV. "We're seeing bright flashes going off all over the sky," Shaw continued.

Those bright flashes were the explosions of Tomahawk cruise missiles striking their targets. The U.S. Navy launched the missiles from warships in the Persian Gulf and Red Sea. Bombs, dropped from warplanes based in Saudi Arabia, rained on Baghdad.

Why were warships and aircraft shelling Iraq? The country was paying the price for invading Kuwait five months earlier. Saddam Hussein, Iraq's president, thought the world would

◀ *Tomahawk cruise missiles from a U.S. Navy warship pound Baghdad.*

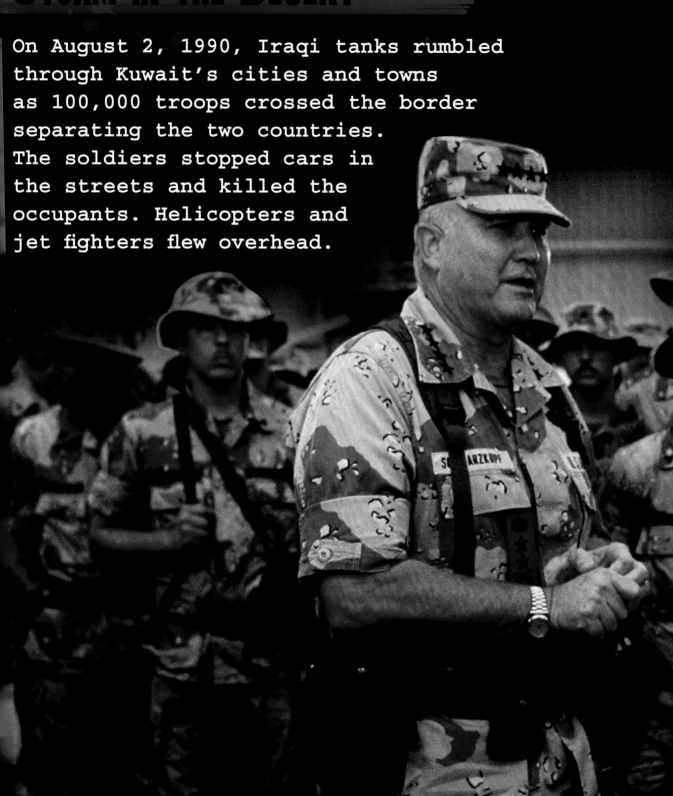

STORM IN THE DESERT

On August 2, 1990, Iraqi tanks rumbled through Kuwait's cities and towns as 100,000 troops crossed the border separating the two countries. The soldiers stopped cars in the streets and killed the occupants. Helicopters and jet fighters flew overhead.

Gen. Norman H. Schwarzkopf III speaks to soldiers inside a hangar while visiting a base camp in the Persian Gulf. Schwarzkopf would lead coalition forces against the Iraqi Army. ▼

The world, including many of Iraq's Arab neighbors, watched in horror. U.S. President George H.W. Bush called Iraq's actions a blatant act of aggression. The United Nations passed a **resolution** calling on Iraq to withdraw. Eventually, Bush persuaded dozens of countries to form a **coalition** to force Iraq to leave Kuwait.

As world leaders tried to find a way to end the crisis, the Iraqis forced the Kuwaitis to become Iraqi citizens. Iraqi soldiers arrested, killed, and tortured thousands.

Slipping into Chaos

Iraq's actions caused the Middle East to slip slowly into chaos. In November, Bush ordered 200,000 U.S. troops to the region. By the end of the year, more than 500,000 coalition troops—stationed on ships at sea and in Saudi Arabia—were within striking distance of Kuwait and Iraq.

For its part, the United Nations set a deadline of midnight (EST) January 15, 1991, for Iraqi troops to withdraw. The deadline came and went. The Iraqis refused to leave. On January 17, at 2:35 a.m. Baghdad time, the bombs began to fall. As the war began, U.S. General H. Norman Schwarzkopf III told his troops: "My confidence in you is total; our cause is just. Now you must be the thunder and lightning of Desert Storm."

LINE IN THE SAND

A Dangerous Region

The exotic deserts of the Middle East have always been fascinating. For many, the region is the cultural, religious, and historical crossroads of the world. It was here that Christianity, Islam, and Judaism flourished. It is also at this intersection that ethnic and religious hatred, colonialism, and the vast riches of the area collided. For centuries, the Middle East has been an extremely volatile place.

That volatility took on new meaning in the 20th century. The French and British drew the boundaries of present-day Iraq when World War I (1914–1918) ended. The French and British, victors of the war, divided Iraq and other Middle Eastern countries, including Kuwait, out of the former old Ottoman Empire (Turkey). After the war, the British protected oil-rich Kuwait. The tiny country declared its independence in 1961.

By the 1990s, the Middle East was at the center of the Cold War, which was a conflict that pitted the Soviet Union and its **allies** against the United States and its friends. Each side poured weapons into the Middle East.

From Boy to Dictator

Born in 1937, Saddam Hussein grew up extremely poor near the Iraqi town of Tikrit. His family lived in a mud hut. As a boy, he stole eggs and chickens for food.

In college, Saddam joined the revolutionary Baath Party. The party's primary goal was to unite all Arabs under one government.

Saddam didn't fare well during his first grab at political power. He fled to Syria in the 1950s after becoming involved in a failed plot to kill Iraqi leader Abdul Karim Kassem. Eventually, Saddam returned to his homeland; and in 1979, he took control of Iraq.

The leader ruled Iraq with an iron fist. Saadam killed and tortured political enemies. In 1980, Saddam ordered a surprise attack on Iraq's neighbor Iran. He thought the war would be over quickly. It ended in a stalemate in 1988.

Saddam Hussein went from poverty to dictator in a short time. He was feared by his enemies and Iraq's neighbors. ▶

THE BUTCHER OF BAGHDAD

Under Saddam Hussein's leadership, Iraq built a massive army of more than a million men and 5,000 tanks. His air force was the most modern in the Middle East. Some of Iraq's military equipment came from the French, the Americans, and the Soviets.

Saddam had missiles that could reach major cities in nearby Israel, Saudi Arabia, and Iran. The Iraqi Army also had chemical and biological weapons. Saddam ordered the use of chemical weapons against Iranian troops and against Kurdish **revolutionaries** in northern Iraq. Many feared Iraq was trying to build a nuclear bomb. Countries throughout the region had good reason to fear the man called the "Butcher of Baghdad."

Eyes on Kuwait

In 1990, Saddam turned his mighty army against Kuwait. He gave varying reasons for the invasion. At first, Saddam said that the Kuwaitis had **revolted** against their rulers and that his army would withdraw once a new Kuwaiti government was in place. Then Saddam said Kuwait was really part of Iraq. Later, Saddam said that if he could not annex Kuwait, he would turn the country into a "graveyard."

The day before the U.N. deadline for the Iraqi Army to leave Kuwait was up, Saddam Hussein inspects his troops in Kuwait. ▶

In reality, Saddam invaded Kuwait to take over its vast oil fields. Kuwait was, and still is, a vastly rich nation, deriving most of its money from the sale of oil to other nations. At the time, Iraq and Kuwait controlled 20 percent of the world's proven oil reserves. Saddam thought that if he controlled Kuwait and its oil, it would not only bring Iraq more riches, but it would increase his standing in the Organization of Petroleum Exporting Countries (OPEC).

Saddam specifically accused Kuwait of stealing from an oil field that ran under both countries. He said Kuwait was waging "economic war" against his country

THE WORLD RESPONDS

Key Blunders

If Saddam Hussein thought he could just take over Kuwait, he was mistaken. The dictator made several key blunders. First, he underestimated the reaction of the British and the Americans. President Bush immediately ordered three aircraft carriers to the region.

Arab Reaction

More importantly, Saddam miscalculated the reaction of fellow Arabs. Immediately after the invasion, Egyptian President Hosni Mubarak called an emergency meeting in Cairo of the Arab League, an association of Arab-speaking countries. Mubarak was angry. Earlier, he had told the world that Iraq would not invade Kuwait, based on personal assurances from Saddam. Mubarak wasn't going to sit still as Iraq swallowed up an Arab neighbor.

During the Cairo meeting, 12 of the league's 20 governments called for Iraq to withdraw immediately from Kuwait and return the emir to power. Member nations also decided to send troops to Saudi Arabia and other Persian Gulf states to protect against another Iraqi attack.

Americans in Los Angeles protest Iraq's occupation of Kuwait. ▼

RE-FREEDOM

FREEDOM FOR THE BALTS

FREE

PEACE IN KUWAIT IRAQ OUT

EMBARGO

The mistakes kept on coming. Saddam Hussein underestimated the reaction of the Soviet Union, his one-time ally. The Soviets supported the Americans and British.

The USS Dwight David Eisenhower was one of several aircraft carriers that the U.S. Navy deployed during the Persian Gulf War. Patrolling in the Red Sea, the Eisenhower stood guard for a possible Iraqi attack on Saudi Arabia. ▶

The Soviets also threw their political weight behind U.N. Security Council Resolution 660, which demanded that the Iraqis leave Kuwait. Three days later, the U.N. Security Council passed Resolution 662, declaring the annexation of Kuwait invalid. On August 6, the U.N. Security Council imposed an economic **embargo**, or ban, on Iraq. This embargo prohibited countries from trading with Iraq, even for oil

Isolated

Throughout late summer and fall of 1990, Saddam became increasingly isolated as the world lined up against him. Because of the embargo, cash-strapped Iraq was growing desperate. Saddam's soldiers plundered Kuwait's riches. They looted shops and homes, stole cars and trucks, seized millions of dollars in foreign currency, and stole millions of gold bars from Kuwaiti banks.

Yet, Saddam was confident that the United States would not respond with its military. He believed Americans would not support a conflict that could turn into another Vietnam War. He expected the United States to seek compromise instead of conflict as the crisis grew.

Saddam was wrong.

BUILDING A COALITION

President Bush was determined from the beginning to force the Iraqis out of Kuwait, either through economic sanctions or military force. Doing nothing was not an option. The strategic and oil-rich Persian Gulf was too important a region.

◀ President George H.W. Bush helped create the largest international coalition to fight a common enemy since World War II. He ordered Iraq to withdraw from Kuwait, which Saddam Hussein ignored.

Within days of the invasion, U.S. warships and those of the Netherlands, Australia, Britain, Canada, France, and Italy sped toward the Persian Gulf. Troops already stationed in the area were put on high alert. "Withdraw from Kuwait unconditionally and immediately, or face the terrible consequences," Bush ordered Iraq's leadership.

Saddam Hussein ignored Bush. In response, Bush drew up a plan to put American ground forces in Saudi Arabia. Most of the Arab world, however, distrusted the United States because of its support of Israel—the enemy of many Arabs.

The Saudis Join the Fray

Bush walked a political and diplomatic tightrope. Saudi Arabia was the holiest of countries in the Islamic world. Any foreign army on Saudi soil might seem to some Muslims as a **desecration** of the Muslim holy land.

Undaunted, Bush sent several officials, including Secretary of Defense Dick Cheney, to meet with Saudi Arabian leaders. The United States wanted to persuade the Saudis to allow American troops in their kingdom. Saudi King Fahd eventually agreed to the American request.

MULTINATIONAL FORCE

The next stage of President Bush's plan was to create the largest military alliance since World War II (1939–1945). While the United States and Great Britain would do the bulk of the fighting, Bush wanted other nations, including those in the Arab world, to join the fight.

Many Arab nations were skeptical. Jordan's King Hussein praised Saddam Hussein. Most Palestinians looked at the Iraqi dictator as a patriot. In the end, 34 nations joined the coalition.

Desert Shield

Never had the world seen such a rapid **deployment** of military might. Code-named Desert Shield, the buildup in the Persian Gulf began in earnest in the fall of 1990. In early November, President Bush ordered another 200,000 troops to the Persian Gulf.

The U.S. Air Force also sent B-52 bombers to Britain and Spain. From those bases, these huge bombers could strike Iraq in a matter of hours. The Turkish government gave its permission for the U.S to base its F-111 fighter planes on Turkish soil.

Family and friends wave good-bye to crew members aboard a U.S. amphibious assault ship as it departs for the Persian Gulf.

Bush tried to resolve the crisis diplomatically as the military moved into position. Saddam seemed eager to talk. Most believed, however, he was just trying to postpone an invasion. Some world diplomats wanted to give economic sanctions time to work. Others wanted the United Nations to offer a compromise to Saddam: that he control a small part of Kuwait but withdraw from the rest of the country.

Troops of the 82nd Airborne Division occupy a trench in Dhahran, Saudi Arabia, as they prepare for war against Iraq. ▼

A MASSIVE BUILDUP

As the clock ticked, President Bush sent Secretary of State James Baker to Switzerland to talk with Iraqi Foreign Minister Tariq Aziz. Baker's message was clear: get out of Kuwait now. Iraq refused. It was clear that the only way to force Saddam Hussein out of Kuwait was at the point of a gun.

The United States and its allies were ready for battle. Not since World War II had there been such a massive sealift and airlift of soldiers, weapons, and cargo. At the end of August, more than 72,000 troops and 100,000 tons of supplies had been airlifted into the region. In total, the United States had 500,000 men and women in the Persian Gulf and its allies had an additional 160,000 troops in the region.

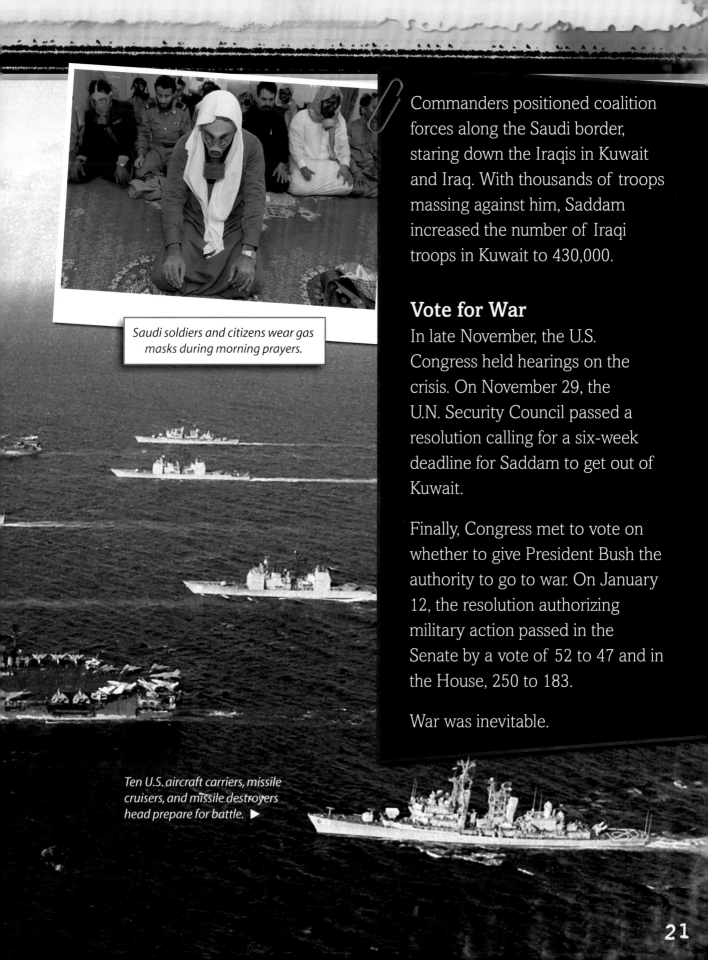

Saudi soldiers and citizens wear gas masks during morning prayers.

Commanders positioned coalition forces along the Saudi border, staring down the Iraqis in Kuwait and Iraq. With thousands of troops massing against him, Saddam increased the number of Iraqi troops in Kuwait to 430,000.

Vote for War

In late November, the U.S. Congress held hearings on the crisis. On November 29, the U.N. Security Council passed a resolution calling for a six-week deadline for Saddam to get out of Kuwait.

Finally, Congress met to vote on whether to give President Bush the authority to go to war. On January 12, the resolution authorizing military action passed in the Senate by a vote of 52 to 47 and in the House, 250 to 183.

War was inevitable.

Ten U.S. aircraft carriers, missile cruisers, and missile destroyers head prepare for battle. ▶

THE WAR BEGINS

Attack from the Air

The world had never seen a war like this. First came bombs from planes. Then came missiles from warships hundreds of miles away. The missiles exploded with video-game accuracy. Millions watched on TV as the war began at about dinnertime in New York City on January 16, 1991. In the Persian Gulf, it was 2:35 a.m., January 17.

With Operation Desert Storm under way, Iraqi anti-aircraft guns fire away hoping to destroy allied aircraft and missiles over the skies of Iraq.

◄ The battleship USS Wisconsin fires at Iraqi targets in Kuwait during Operation Desert Storm. The Wisconsin also launched Tomahawk cruise missiles, the first time the missiles were used in combat.

From the beginning, the United States used massive firepower and overwhelming force to paralyze the Iraqi Army. The first U.S. warplanes in the air that night were the supersecret F-117 Stealth fighters. Engineers designed these sleek attack aircraft to avoid enemy radar detection. They dropped computer-guided smart bombs with lethal accuracy.

In the Crosshairs

The first weapon to score a direct hit on Baghdad that night was another technological marvel, the Tomahawk land attack cruise missile. Designed to fly up to 550 miles per hour, the Tomahawk zoomed just above the ground at 100 feet. Its speed and ability to fly this low made the missile invisible to enemy radar and antiaircraft fire.

AIR CONTROL

Quickly the Americans and their allies gained the upper hand in the air. They knocked out Iraq's radar and antiaircraft defenses. They also aimed for Iraq's communication centers and government buildings. The goal was to make the Iraqi commanders blind by disrupting communication between them and their troops.

Some of the first targets were pinpoint surgical strikes against the Defense Ministry and Baath Party headquarters. Bombs and missiles also scored direct hits on the Iraqi Communications Center, the Republican Palace, Iraq's Parliament building, and the airport. In addition, allied airplanes and warships targeted missile sites and bridges in Iraq and Kuwait.

Desert Storm

Although the allies had superior technology and weapons, the first day of the war did not come without casualties. The Iraqis shot down four aircraft that day: one from the U.S. Navy, two from the Royal Air Force, and one Kuwaiti airship. U.S. fighters destroyed eight Iraqi aircraft in air-to-air combat.

▲ *British Tornado F3 fighters fly over the battlefield.*

Soldiers load bombs onto an aircraft as they ready it for a mission.

Hours after the air war had begun, Marlin Fitzwater, President Bush's press secretary, read a statement from the commander in chief: "The liberation of Kuwait has begun." Operation Desert Shield was now Operation Desert Storm.

When asked what would happen to the Iraqi Army in Kuwait, Colin Powell, chairman of the Joint Chiefs of Staff, said: "First we're going to cut it off, then we're going to kill it."

Cruise missiles being fired from a warship at sea. These missiles carried a 1,000-pound, high-explosive warhead.

SADDAM STRIKES BACK

Scuds Start Flying

Saddam wasn't going to sit back as the allies turned Iraq into rubble. But what could he do? Iraq's antiaircraft defense system was worthless against such high-tech weapons. Furthermore, coalition bombs all but destroyed Saddam's air force. Many of Iraq's jet fighters never got off the ground. Ever defiant, Saddam planned a counterattack—against Israel.

Saddam believed if he could draw Israel into the war, many Arab countries would leave the U.N. coalition. During the early morning hours of January 17, the Iraqis launched their first Soviet-made Scud missile against Israel. Scuds were not accurate weapons. Once launched, no one knew where the missile would hit. At about 2 a.m., the first Scud slammed into Tel Aviv.

Patriots to the Rescue

News reports showed a panicked city. Fearing that Saddam would arm the missiles with biological or chemical weapons, residents, children, and reporters donned gas masks. Israeli leaders had said earlier that they would **retaliate** if Iraq attacked. But once the Scuds started falling, the United States urged the Israelis not to strike back. Israel agreed

The United States deployed its ultrasophisticated Patriot Air Defense System. Flying three to five times the speed of sound, a Patriot missile could strike an incoming missile with deadly accuracy. The Scud was no match for the Patriot.

Fearing a chemical missile attack from Iraq, many Israelis donned gas masks.

◄ *Smoke cascades over Tel Aviv after the Israeli city was struck by an Iraqi Scud missile. Iraq had hoped to draw Israel into the war. Saddam Hussein thought that if Israel joined the allies, other Arab states would withdraw from the coalition.*

SADDAM HUSSEIN EYES SAUDI ARABIA

Saddam also launched Scud missiles against Saudi Arabia. Once again, Saddam miscalculated. By attacking Saudi Arabia, the Arab world pulled further away from Iraq.

Soldiers standing near the debris after a Scud missile heavily damaged a sector of
▼ a city during Operation Desert Storm.

An American soldier walks through the rubble of a U.S. military barrack after an Iraqi scud missile destroyed the structure the night before. The attack killed 28 soldiers and wounded more than 100 others.

The most **lethal** Scud attack occurred when a missile slammed into the city of Dhahran. The missile exploded over the **barracks** of an Army Reserve unit from Greensburg, Pennsylvania. Twenty-eight soldiers died in the blast and more than one hundred were wounded. Iraq launched a total of 86 Scuds during the war—46 against Saudi Arabia and 40 at Israel.

Aircrews Captured

Although Iraq wasn't winning the air war, the Iraqis tried to elicit sympathy from the world with **propaganda**. The Iraqis paraded captured airmen in front of TV cameras and forced the prisoners to denounce the war.

Once again, Saddam got it wrong. Instead of winning sympathy, the world **condemned** Saddam's mistreatment of prisoners.

THE 100-HOUR WAR

The Ground War Begins

Death came in the form of submarine-launched Tomahawk cruise missiles and laser-guided smart bombs. During six hectic weeks, allied forces flew 3,000 missions a day and dropped 90,000 tons of bombs.

U.S. commanders used the air war to weaken Iraqi defenses. By late February, military commanders and President Bush thought the air strikes had done enough damage.

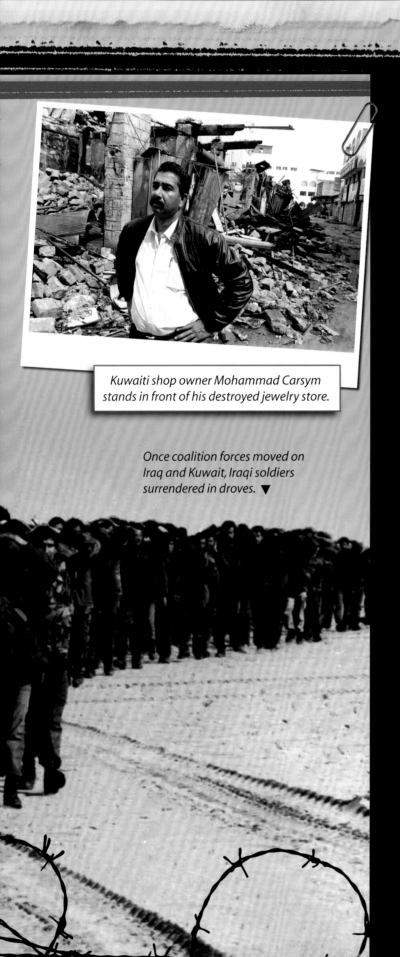

Kuwaiti shop owner Mohammad Carsym stands in front of his destroyed jewelry store.

Once coalition forces moved on Iraq and Kuwait, Iraqi soldiers surrendered in droves. ▼

"Mother of All Battles"

Now it was time to put the second phase of Desert Storm into action. At 4 a.m. on Monday, February 24, ground troops rolled into Iraq and Kuwait. General Schwarzkopf feared that if the allies hit the Iraqis head-on behind their fortifications, the enemy would kill and injure thousands of his troops.

Instead, Schwarzkopf ordered 200,000 French, British, and American troops north into the Iraqi desert. He then had them curl east toward the port city of Al Basrah. At the same time, allied troops marched toward Kuwait City from southern Saudi Arabia. This maneuver trapped Iraqi forces in Kuwait and in southern Iraq.

As allied troops stormed across the border, the Iraqis set Kuwaiti oil fields on fire. In Kuwait City, the Iraqis shot civilians and detained thousands. In just 10 hours, though, coalition troops captured 5,000 Iraqi soldiers. The Iraqis didn't put up much of a fight. By the second day of the ground offensive, 30,000 Iraqi troops had laid down their arms.

LIBERATED!

As the Iraqi
Army crumbled,
the allies
pushed on toward
Kuwait City. By
Tuesday, February
25, the allies had thrown the Iraqi
Army out of Kuwait. Saudi and Kuwaiti
troops then marched into Kuwait City
on Wednesday. As the Iraqis retreated,
they set fire to 600 oil wells, burning
5 million gallons of oil a day.
Kuwait's cities were in shambles.

*As Iraqi troops retreated across Kuwait,
they set oil fields afire. Thick, black, toxic
smoke billowed for weeks.* ▼

At 5 a.m. on Thursday, February 27, President Bush announced an end to the fighting. After 100 hours, the ground war was over. The allies had accomplished the goal of **liberating** Kuwait and driving Iraq from the battlefield. "Kuwait is liberated," Bush announced the next day. "Iraq's military is defeated. Our military objectives are met."

Hostilities End

With that announcement, coalition troops did not conquer Baghdad as many had hoped. Instead, Saddam Hussein remained in power. Iraq and the allies signed the formal cease-fire agreement on Sunday, March 3.

At the war's end, U.S. casualties totaled 148 battle deaths, 145 non-battle deaths, and 467 Americans were wounded. An estimated 100,000 Iraqi soldiers died; 300,000 were injured; approximately 150,000 **deserted**, or left, the army; and allied forces captured more than 65,000.

AFTERMATH

A U.S. soldier embraces a loved one after returning home from the Persian Gulf War. Many communities across the United States held parades and ceremonies in honor of the troops. ▼

No More Vietnams

Not since the Spanish American War (1898) had the United States won a conflict so quickly and handily. Some Americans had feared that the United States would be bogged down in another unwinnable war, such as Vietnam. That did not occur.

In the end, the Persian Gulf War was short and popular. It underscored that a new age of high-tech warfare had dawned. The war caused many countries that distrusted one another to come together. It also strengthened American ties to the region.

Gulf War Syndrome

But a dark side soon emerged. Many allied soldiers returned home from Iraq sick. Their symptoms ranged from tiredness, dizziness, loss of memory, muscle and joint pain to immune system problems. Soldiers and doctors now refer to these symptoms as the Gulf War syndrome.

More than 15 years after the war, no one knows why the troops became sick. No one can say how many soldiers returned home from Iraq sick.

THE IMPACT OF SANCTIONS

Saddam Hussein fared well after the war. He remained in power while U.S. troops stayed behind in Saudi Arabia and Kuwait. The allies formed a "no-fly zone" in Iraq. The zone, patrolled by allied warplanes, protected the Kurds in northern Iraq and Shiite Muslims in the south from Iraqi warplanes.

The United Nations continued its economic sanctions. The United States had hoped that the sanctions would force a revolt in Iraq, which would end Saddam's rule.

Another War

Saddam had to disarm in order for the United Nations to lift the sanctions. The United States and other countries believed Saddam was **stockpiling** chemical and biological weapons. They also feared Saddam was still trying to build a nuclear bomb. In 2003, U.N. weapons inspectors argued that Saddam didn't have any weapons of mass destruction.

U.S. officials argued that Iraq still posed a threat. Most countries were skeptical. Nevertheless, the United States, Britain, and a handful of other nations invaded Iraq on March 20, 2003. That coalition finally ousted Saddam from power. The new Iraqi government eventually put Saddam on trial and executed the "Butcher of Baghdad" for crimes he had committed as Iraq's leader.

The United States did not find any weapons of mass destruction. In 2008, the United States was still fighting in Iraq.

Saddam Hussein survived the Persian Gulf War, but he wouldn't be so lucky in 2003 when another U.S.-led coalition invaded Iraq and ousted the dictator from power. The Butcher of Baghdad would later be executed for war crimes. ▶

37

GLOSSARY

allies—friends

annex—to take control of

barracks—where soldiers sleep and live

coalition—temporary union for a common purpose

colonialism—the control by one power over an area or a people

condemned—declared to be evil or wrong

deployment—the act of spreading out, as in the movement of troops and ships for battle

desecration—to ruin

deserted—left without permission

embargo—ban

exotic—unfamiliar, unusual

lethal—deadly

liberating—setting free

propaganda—the spreading of ideas or information to further or damage a cause

retaliate—to fight back

resolution—formal statement expressing the opinion, or will, of a legislative body

revolted—refused to support a ruler or government

revolutionaries—those who take part in a revolution or revolt

sanctions— coercive measures adopted, usually by several nations in cooperation, to force another nation violating international law to stop or yield to adjudication

stockpiling—putting away supplies for future use

volatile—explosive, tense, tending to erupt into violence

SOURCES

Books

CNN War in the Gulf, Turner Publishing, Inc., Atlanta Georgia, 1991.

Desert Storm, The War in the Persian Gulf; the Editors of Time Magazine,
Time Warner Publishing Inc., 1991.

Triumph in the Desert, Peter David, Random House, New York, 1991.

Web Sites

Academy of Achievement
General H. Norman Schwarzkoph
http://www.achievement.org/autodoc/page/sch0bio-1
General Colin L. Powell

http://www.achievement.org/autodoc/page/pow0bio-1

CNN The Unfinished War: A Decade Since Desert Storm
http://www.cnn.com/SPECIALS/2001/gulf.war/facts/gulfwar/
Federation of American Scientists Military Analysis Network: F-117A Nighthawk
http://www.fas.org/man/dod-101/sys/ac/f-117.htm
Frontline: The Gulf War. Weapons
http://www.pbs.org/wgbh/pages/frontline/gulf/weapons/scud.html
Frontline: An Interview with Tariq Aziz

http://www.pbs.org/wgbh/pages/frontline/shows/saddam/interviews/aziz.html

How Stuff Works
How Smart Bombs Work
http://science.howstuffworks.com/smart-bomb.htm

Women in the Military Service For America Memorial Foundation
http://chnm.gmu.edu/courses/rr/s01/cw/students/leeann/historyandcollections/
collections/photopages/phespersgulf.html

INDEX